ZLATA'S DIARY

by

Zlata Filipovic

Student Packet

Written by

Stacie Lee Champlin Dreibrodt

Contains masters for:

2 Prereading Activities
1 Study Guide (4 pages)
7 Vocabulary Activities
4 Critical Thinking Activities
1 Literary Analysis Activity
2 Writing Activities
2 Comprehension Quizzes
1 Final Test
1 Essay Evaluation Form

Plus Detailed Answer Key

Note

The Penguin paperback edition of this book published by Penguin Books Ltd, ©1994, was used to prepare this guide. Page references may differ in other editions.

Please note: This novel deals with the issue of war. Please assess the appropriateness of this book for the age level and maturity of your students prior to reading and discussing it with your class.

ISBN 1-58130-705-5

Printed in the United States of America.

To order, contact your local school supply store, or—

Novel Units, Inc.
P.O. Box 97
Bulverde, TX 78163-0097

Web site: www.educyberstor.com

Name ________________________________

Directions: Consider the following statements. Create a journal to respond to various issues throughout the story. Write your responses to these statements in the journal. Re-evaluate these statements after reading the story.

1. Children in other countries live exactly as you do.
2. War always involves two active parties.
3. If there is no shooting, there is no war.
4. War is a necessary evil.
5. The main result of war is that it is dangerous to go out into the streets.
6. If you keep to yourself, you are basically unaffected by the war outside.
7. Everyone deserves a childhood.
8. Once you leave the war behind, you can go on with your regular life.
9. Money is the solution to difficulties during war.
10. Only those directly involved with the war are ever injured or killed.

Name ______________________________

Zlata's Diary
Activity #2 • Initiating Activity
Use Before Reading

Directions: Think about each idea listed below. Then freewrite about each idea for at least five minutes. Use extra paper if necessary. Be prepared to share your thoughts with your classmates.

1. family

2. freedom

3. electricity

4. childhood

5. war

Develop your thoughts on one of the topics. Use this page to brainstorm ideas for an essay.

Name ______________________________

Introduction–February 4, Pages *v*-23

1. What does Zlata call her diary?
2. What happens to Zlata's friend, Nina?
3. Describe Zlata's life prior to the spring of 1992.
4. Describe Zlata's life after the spring of 1992.
5. Why was Zlata upset each time one of the journalists left?
6. Why is it that Zlata seemed like such an adult?
7. For whom does Janine Di Giovanni claim that Zlata wrote this book?
8. What does Zlata tell us in the first diary entry?
9. Why are we told that Zlata's father was called off to duty?

February 15–June 1, Pages 24-53

1. Who are the "kids"?
2. Why doesn't Zlata's class go to the music concert?
3. What is beginning to happen in Sarajevo?
4. If this were to occur in your hometown, what would happen?
5. Why does Mommy pack Zlata's suitcase?
6. How does Zlata feel about the war and how long it will last?

June 5–September 21, Pages 54-83

1. What happened to the family's country house?
2. What happened to their neighbors?
3. Who does Zlata claim is her family?
4. Who is Cici?
5. Why is it so hard to live without water and electricity?
6. Who does Zlata credit for helping during these difficult times?
7. How long does Zlata go without seeing her grandparents during the war?

Name ______________________________

8. Describe some of the birthday presents Zlata's family gives to each other. Is there anything strange about the gifts? Why or why not?
9. Describe in your own words what Zlata's life is now like.

September 28–January 15, Pages 84-115

1. Who comes to visit Zlata?
2. Why is it that they only talk about the war?
3. What is going to happen to Mimmy?
4. Where are Zlata and her mother going?
5. What is happening to all of the trees?
6. What happened to Braco's friend?
7. How does Zlata feel about politics and "young" people?
8. Summarize the conditions in Sarajevo.
9. What could you do to help someone in Zlata's condition?
10. What does Zlata's behavior at the Christmas party tell you about her?
11. How does Zlata feel about leaving her father and grandparents?

January 24–May 20, Pages 116-141

1. Why doesn't Zlata's family have their electricity turned back on? What do they do about it?
2. Why are birthdays so special?
3. What does Zlata think about the convoy?
4. Why is Zlata afraid that Cicko might die? What is the solution?
5. Zlata is able to start school again; why is she so happy about that?
6. What does Zlata's mother's reaction to Cicko's death say about her character?
7. What has Zlata decided about the war?
8. The neighborhood seems to take care of each other. Is this normal, or is it due to the circumstances?

Name ______________________________

9. How are the "kids" planning on dividing the people of Sarajevo?
10. What happened in the house that makes Mommy scared and uncomfortable?
11. What is Nedo going to do?
12. Does Daddy think that Nedo will return to Sarajevo? Why or why not?

May 25–August 26, Pages 142-168

1. What will happen to Zlata's diary entries?
2. Why can't the family keep the puppy?
3. What is Nedo going to do?
4. Why do letters from her friends mean so much to Zlata?
5. Do you think good things always happen to good people? Why or why not?
6. Identify the metaphors in Zlata's message that she read at the promotion.
7. Why can't the journalists do something to help Zlata and the people of Sarajevo?
8. Why does it frighten Zlata to be compared to Anne Frank?
9. What happened to Cici? Why is Zlata upset?
10. Explain why Mommy and Daddy keep telling Zlata that "after the clouds comes the sun."
11. Why does Zlata say that they must "steel themselves"?

August 27–Epilogue, Pages 169-197

1. In your own words, explain how Zlata must feel to see all of her friends leaving Sarajevo.
2. Why does the loss of the mail have such an impact on Zlata?
3. What is supposed to happen on September 21?
4. Why does Zlata say that the war should end?
5. How many people have died? been injured?
6. What happens to the notion of peace?
7. What was supposed to happen on December 8, 1993?

Name ______________________________

8. What does happen on December 8?
9. What happens on December 22, 1993?
10. How does Zlata feel about the lights of Paris?
11. Why does Zlata say that she cannot claim or enjoy the lights of Paris?

Name ______________________________

barricades (*v*)	irrevocably (*v*)	artillery (*vi*)	shrapnel (*vi*)
cowering (*vii*)	humanitarian (*vii*)	diligent (*vii*)	resigned (*ix*)
stoical (*ix*)	notorious (*x*)	traumatized (*xii*)	solfeggio (1)
herbarium (4)	politics (6)	antibiotic (12)	pessimist (13)
inspiration (13)	persistent (14)	proverbial (17)	epidemic (23)

Directions: Create a crossword puzzle that will include each of the above words. When you write clues, try to use something other than the word-for-word definition. Be creative. Find a partner when you are finished. Try to solve each other's crossword puzzle.

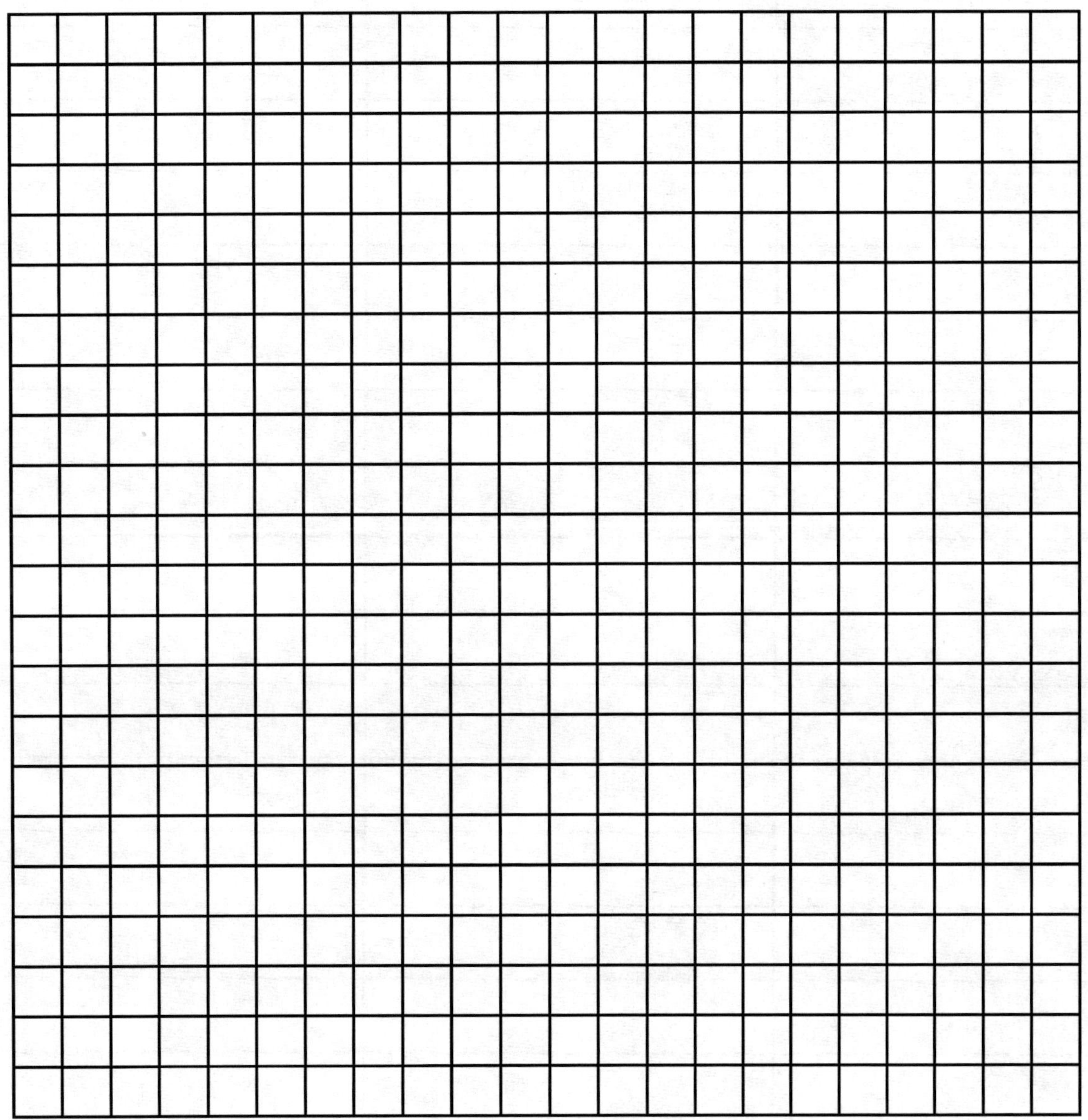

Name ______________________________

civilians (24) procession (24) parliament (24) barracks (24)
Muslim (29) humanity (33) revolting (35) amputate (47)
dismembered (51) hysterically (51)

Directions: Use the vocabulary words from the list. Write each one in the middle column of the chart. Write an antonym for each word in the left-hand column. Write a synonym for each word in the right-hand column.

Antonym	Vocabulary Word	Synonym

Name ______________________________

barrage (56)	servile (59)	humiliating (59)	liberated (66)
intervention (66)	pedigree (68)	sovereign (70)	hernia (74)

Directions: Match each sentence to the appropriate vocabulary word. Then use the line to write a new sentence using the vocabulary word.

1. Help, Mom, Joey keeps annoying me!

   ____

2. Our dog is a full-bred Cocker Spaniel.

   ____

3. Please don't show everyone that terrible picture right after I lost all of my teeth.

   ____

4. I am your king, and you are my followers.

   ____

5. I can do it all by myself.

   ____

6. You act as if I should do everything for you, including your chores.

   ____

7. That is too heavy to lift; don't hurt yourself.

   ____

8. Every time I try to cross the yard, I get hit with snowballs.

   ____

Name ______________________________

convoy (84)	negotiating (85)	idiocy (95)	philosophizing (97)
condemned (98)	Adventist (111)		

Directions: Use at least five of the vocabulary words in a paragraph describing life during wartime. Try to paint a vivid picture of what life might be like.

Name ______________________________

priority (116)	kilt (116)	cardigan (116)	marzipan (117)
refugees (122)	invalids (124)	radiation (126)	fortified (133)

Directions: Write each vocabulary word in the chart below, along with its part of speech. Use each word in a sentence; then identify the related word, part of speech, and write a definition. One has been done for you.

Vocabulary Word	Sentence	Related Word	Part of Speech	Definition
1. kilt (noun)	In Scotland many men wear kilts.	skirt	noun	type of clothing

Name ______________________________

inventive (159) optimistic (165) demilitarization (165) suppressing (168)

Directions: Create a word map for each of the vocabulary words listed above. Display the finished products in the classroom.

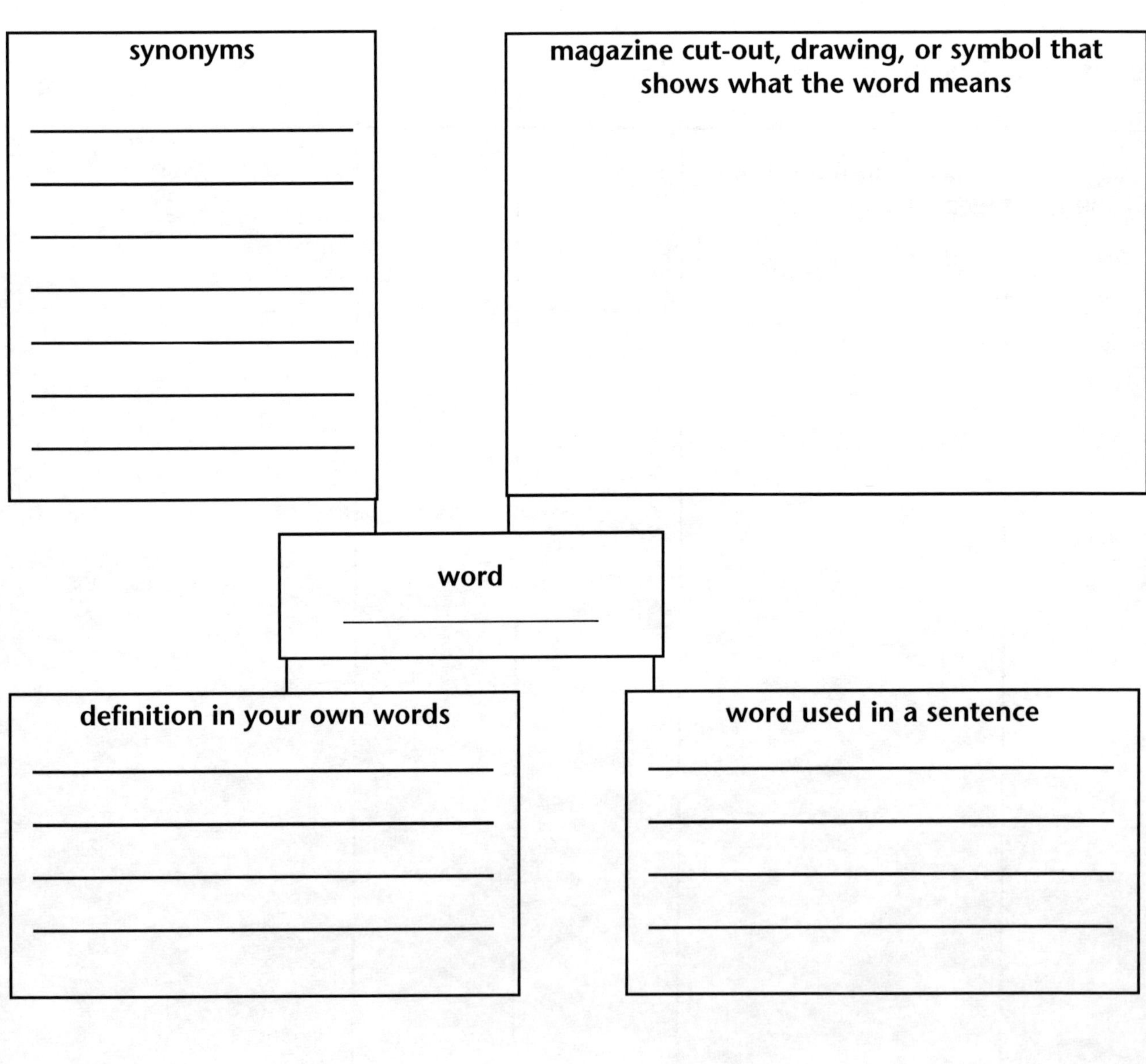

Name ________________________________

lodgers (169)	demolished (170)	enriched (170)	trove (171)
deteriorating (173)	obligations (173)	archive (175)	truces (177)
rationed (179)	illuminates (197)		

Directions: Write each vocabulary word in the correct column below.

Noun	Verb	Adjective or Adverb
♣	❁	▲
❖	■	✖
✻	♣	❤
♦	❀	❁
❁	▲	✻
▲	♦	❀
■	❖	♦
❀	✖	♣
❤	✻	■
✖	❤	❖

Find sets of words with the same symbols. For example, the three words written beside the ♣ form a set. On a separate sheet of paper, write a sentence that includes each set of words.

Name ______________________________

Zlata's Diary
Activity #10 • Critical Thinking
Use After Reading

Understanding Values

Directions: Values represent people's beliefs about what is important, good, or worthwhile. For example, most families consider spending time together as very important—it is something they value.

Think about the following characters from *Zlata's Diary* and the values they have: Zlata, Mommy, Daddy, the "kids," Nedo, Braco. What do they value? What beliefs do they have about what is important, good, or worthwhile? On the chart below, list each character's three most important values, from most important to least. Be prepared to share your lists during a class discussion.

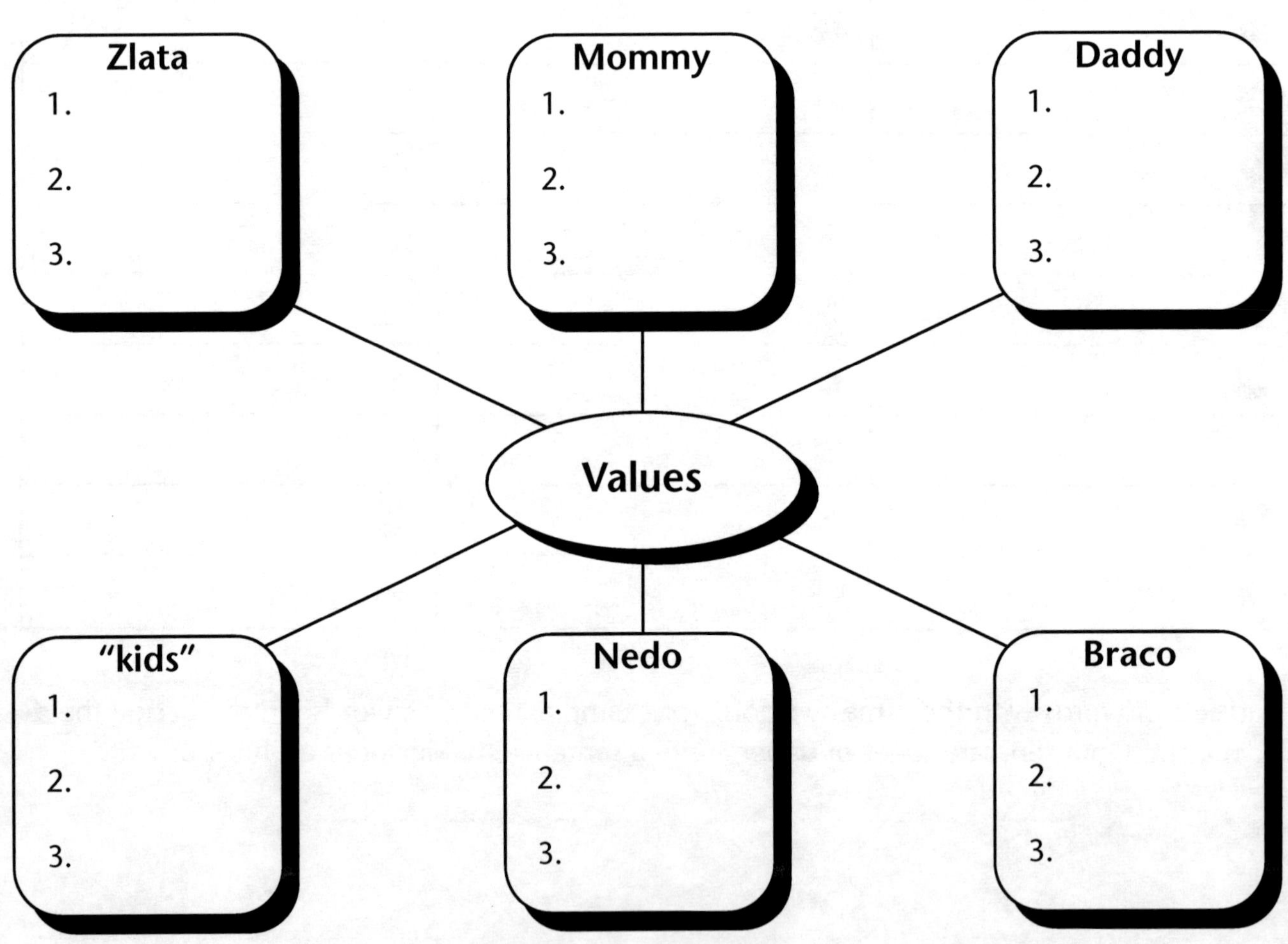

After you have finished the chart and participated in the class discussion, think about which character seems to have values most like your own. Write a paragraph that explains why you chose this character.

Name ______________________________

Conflict

The **conflict** of a story is the struggle between two people or two forces. There are three main types of conflict: person against person, person against nature or society, and person against himself/herself.

Directions: The characters in *Zlata's Diary* experience some conflicts in the story. In the chart below, list the names of three major characters. In the space provided, list a conflict each character experienced. Then explain how each conflict is resolved in the story.

Character:

Conflict	Resolution

Character:

Conflict	Resolution

Character:

Conflict	Resolution

Name ______________________________

Survival Chart

Directions: Imagine that your hometown was suddenly ravaged by war. What would you do to protect yourself and your family? What items would be most necessary for your survival? List all of the items that you think you and your family would need. Explain the rationale behind each item. You are limited to ten items.

Items	Rationale for Including Item
1.	
2.	
3.	
4.	
5.	
6.	
7.	
8.	
9.	
10.	

Name ________________________________

Zlata's Diary
Activity #13 • Character Analysis
Use After Reading

Feelings

Directions: Examine how Zlata has changed from the early to the later entries in her diary. Describe key events and how Zlata might have felt as these events occurred. How does she change? Why?

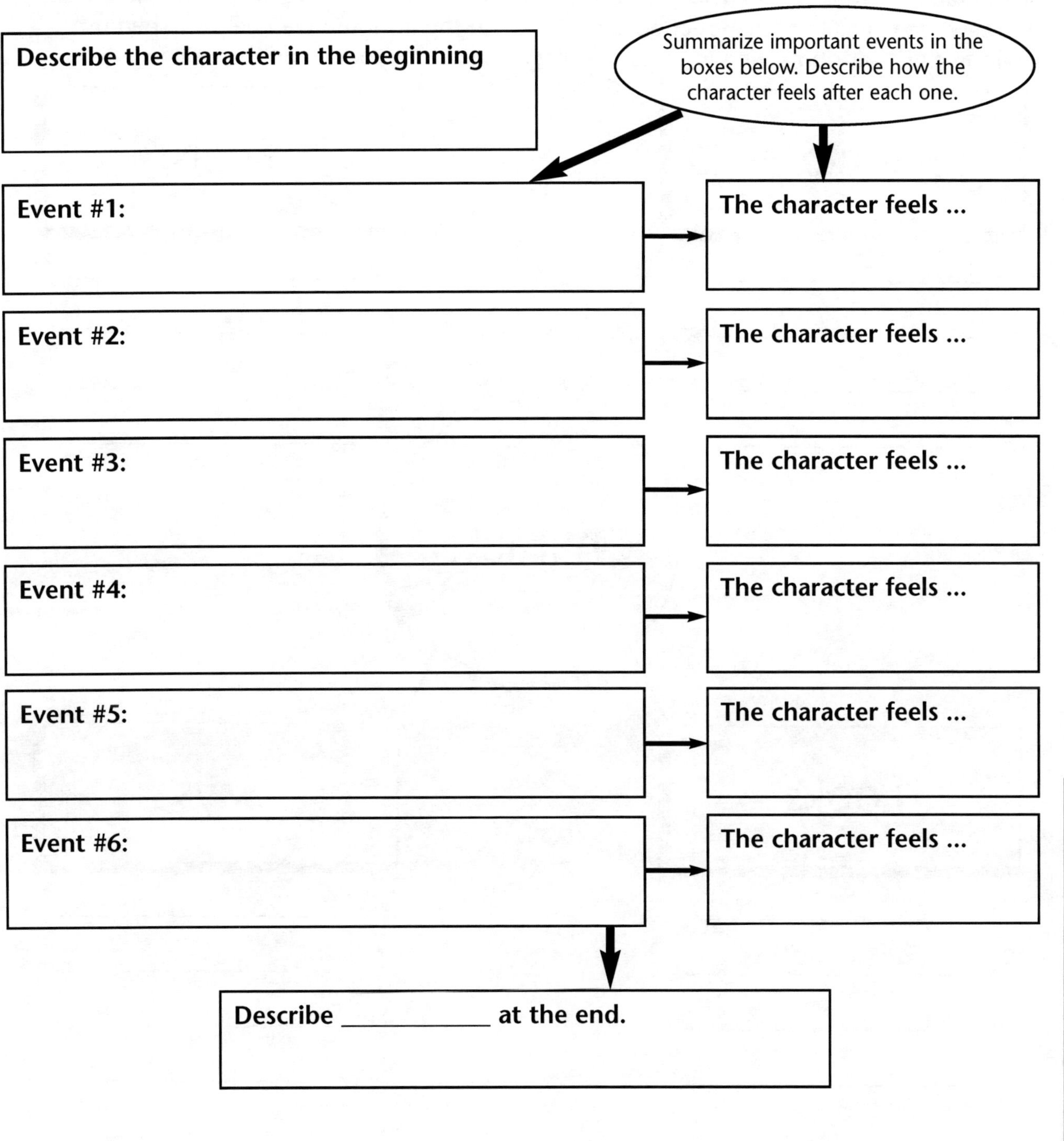

Name ______________________________

Character Sketch

Directions: Think about the characters in *Zlata's Diary*. Which character is your favorite? Why? List this character's qualities on the attribute web. (You may have made attribute webs for several characters as you read the book. If so, use information recorded from these webs to review the characters and select qualities to list on the attribute web below.) Then use details from the attribute web to write a character sketch of your favorite character.

Acts

1. ______________________
2. ______________________
3. ______________________
4. ______________________

Feels

1. ______________________
2. ______________________
3. ______________________
4. ______________________

Character

Looks

1. ______________________
2. ______________________
3. ______________________
4. ______________________

Says

1. ______________________
2. ______________________
3. ______________________
4. ______________________

Name ______________________________

Sociogram

Directions: On the lines, use one word to describe the relationship between Zlata and other people in *Zlata's Diary.* Remember that relationships go both ways and that each line needs a descriptive word. Seven characters have been filled in for you. Add other characters to the sociogram and describe their relationship with Zlata.

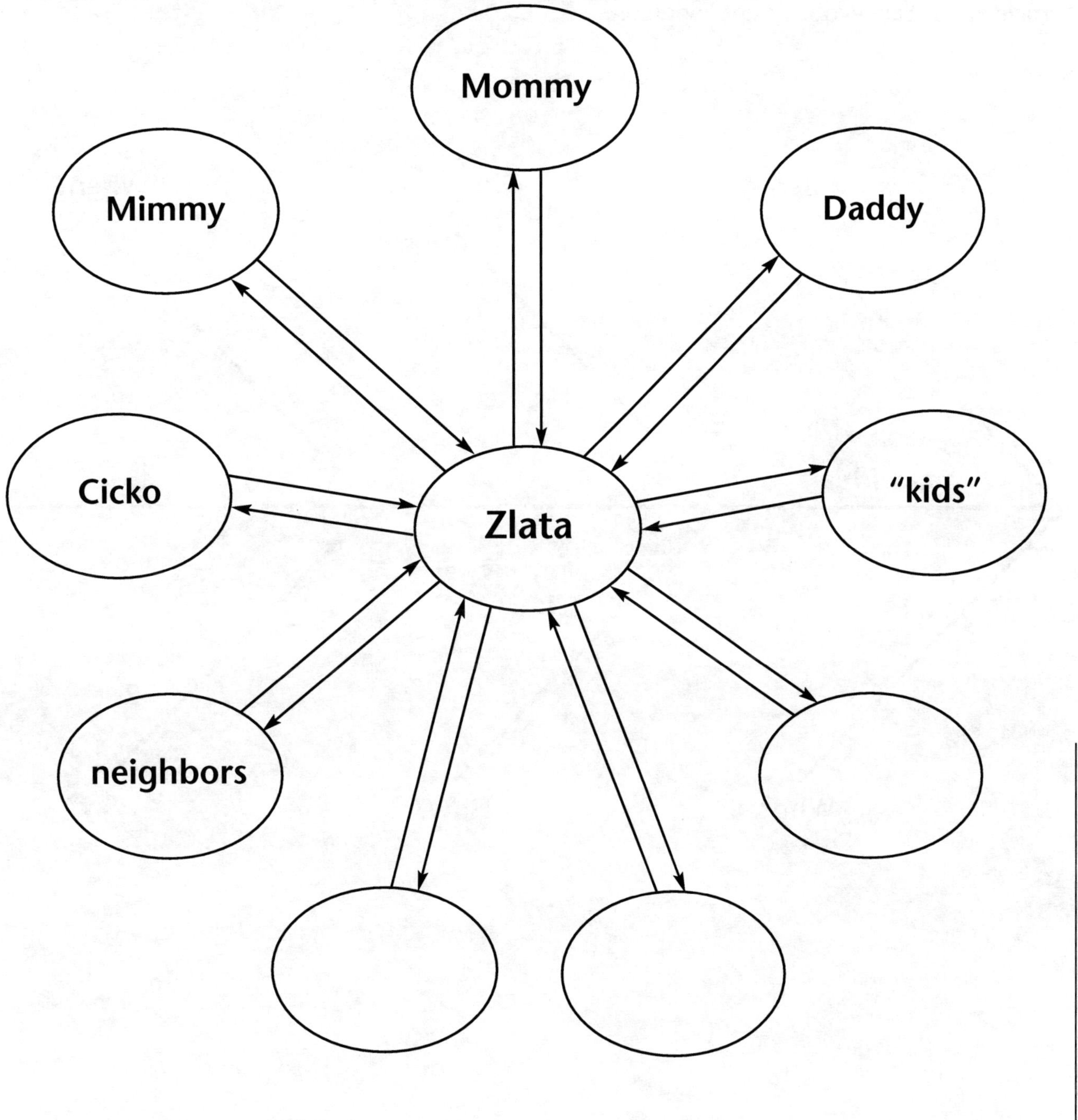

Name ______________________________

Herringbone

Directions: Find out some information about the condition of Sarajevo today. How has it changed? Has the war ended? What happened to all of the refugees? Did they ever return home? How has Sarajevo changed forever? What other countries have suffered this same fate? Add spaces if there are more than two answers to a question. Then write a newspaper article about Sarajevo's current condition.

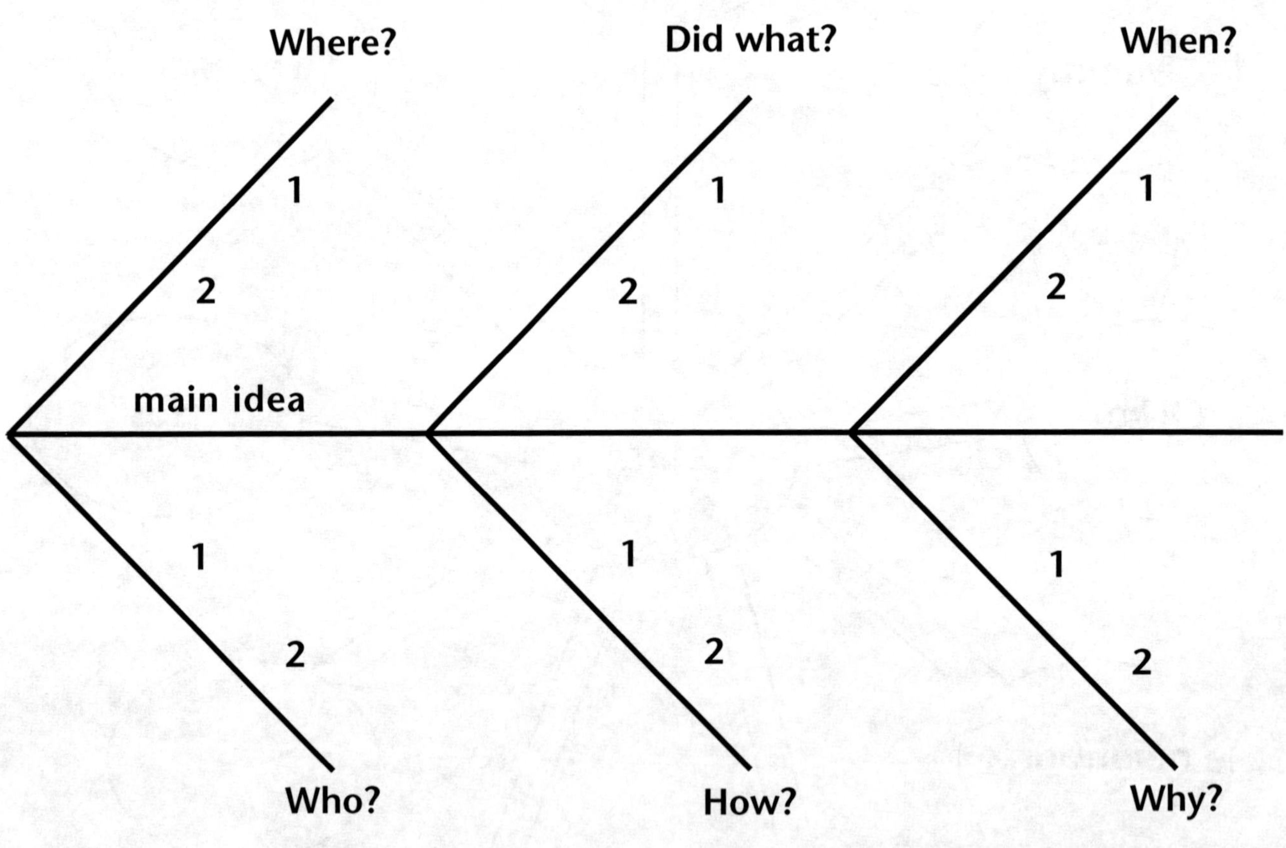

Name ______________________________

Directions: Mark the following statements True (T) or False (F). If the statement is false, correct it so that it is true.

_____ 1. Zlata's family is able to prepare for the war.

_____ 2. During the war the family goes without electricity for extended periods of time.

_____ 3. Zlata does not know anyone who is killed during the war.

_____ 4. Some people send their children to other countries so that they will not have to care for them.

_____ 5. There are not enough buses to hold all of the people wishing to leave Sarajevo.

_____ 6. In war, only those who are directly involved in the fighting are injured or killed.

_____ 7. Zlata's neighborhood becomes her family.

_____ 8. Zlata wishes that the neighbors would learn to help one another.

_____ 9. Zlata is allowed to play outside for only one hour each day.

_____ 10. Mimmy was taken and destroyed by the soldiers.

Name ______________________________

Directions: Mark the following statements True (T) or False (F). If the statement is false, correct it so that it is true.

_____ 1. Zlata is never able to get used to the war going on around her.

_____ 2. Cicko escapes from the cage and flies away.

_____ 3. Zlata refers to the politicians as the "kids."

_____ 4. Zlata trusts that the "kids" will come to an agreement.

_____ 5. Daddy reassures Zlata that Nedo will return from his vacation.

_____ 6. Zlata is concerned by how much the war is aging her parents.

_____ 7. Zlata is optimistic that the war will soon end.

_____ 8. Zlata is thrilled to be compared to Anne Frank.

_____ 9. Mommy and Daddy try to tell Zlata that things will get better.

_____ 10. Zlata's family relocates to Paris.

Name ______________________________

A. Short Answer: Answer the following questions with short answers (two or three sentences).

1. How does Zlata feel about the idea of leaving Sarajevo?

2. What things does Zlata do in order to survive each day?

3. Why does Zlata feel so alone?

4. Describe Zlata in your own words.

5. What type of circumstances is Zlata living in?

6. How does Zlata feel about the "kids"?

7. How does Zlata feel about going to school?

8. Describe Zlata's birthdays during wartime.

9. Why does Zlata hate the idea that items are sold for foreign money?

10. Why does Zlata have a hard time accepting the luxuries in Paris?

Name ________________________________

B. Identification: Explain the importance of each one of the following items to Zlata and the story.

1. Mimmy

2. War

3. Peace

4. Electricity

5. Family

6. Cici and Cicko

7. School

Name ______________________________

8. Childhood

9. Death

10. Gas

11. Birthdays

12. Cellars

13. Radios

14. the "kids"

15. Books

Name ______________________________

C. Essays: Pick three of the following essays to answer. Be sure to include information from the book to support your answers.

1. Consider Zlata's life before, during, and after the war. How does her life change over the course of about three years? What major events occur that shape her into the person she becomes? Does the war change her in a positive or a negative way? Support your answer with evidence from the text.

2. Do you agree or disagree with the statement that war is a necessary evil? Explain why or why not. What would the world be like without war? How would our history be different? Use examples from the book in your response.

3. Write a letter to Zlata expressing your reaction to her story. Tell Zlata how her story has changed your thoughts and ideas.

4. Pretend that you are Zlata. What are the main lessons or ideas that you wish to share with the world through your story? Explain the importance of these lessons and why you would include them.

5. Zlata keeps saying that her childhood has been taken from her. How important is it to have a childhood? How different would you be if you were never able to act like a child? Will this affect Zlata positively or negatively in the future?

Answer Key

Activities #1 & #2: Accept reasonable answers.
Study Questions—Pages *v*-23: 1. Mimmy 2. She is killed while playing in the park. 3. Her family was well-off; they had a nice apartment and a country home. 4. Her parents no longer work; they lose weight. They have no food, water, electricity, or school. 5. Due to the loss of most of her friends, she attached herself to anyone she met. 6. She has seen so much and she must also be strong for her parents. 7. for all of the children who are not safe 8. She is starting fifth grade, and she is anxious to see her friends again. 9. foreshadowing
Pages 24-53 : 1. politicians 2. It is too dangerous. 3. People are being shot and killed; schools are closed. 4. Answers will vary. 5. She might be leaving. 6. She thinks it will stop soon.
Pages 54-83: 1. It burnt down. 2. They were killed. 3. her neighborhood 4. a kitten Nedo found 5. Answers will vary. 6. her friends, Maja, Bojana, and Nedo 7. four months 8. coffee, stockings, shampoo, tie rack; They have to give whatever they can find. Those items are luxuries at the moment. 9. She is stuck inside and is afraid to go outside. Many of her friends have left. They have no food, water, or electricity. They are happy for every day that they have.
Pages 84-115: 1. Mirna 2. Answers will vary. 3. The diary is going to be published. 4. Holland 5. They have been condemned and are probably being sold for foreign money in the markets. 6. He was killed while they were trying to escape. 7. Politics are conducted by grown-ups, but the "young" could have done better. The young people never would have chosen war. 8. Answers will vary. 9. Answers will vary. 10. She is a nice, caring person; Answers will vary. 11. She is scared, but she is tired of the war.
Pages 116-141: 1. They are not priority customers; their neighbor allows them to use some of their electricity. 2. It is a chance for friends and family to gather; it is an escape from war and politics. 3. She doesn't think that they will ever be allowed to leave. 4. He runs out of birdseed; other people bring some for him. 5. It will give her something to do, and take her mind off the situation. 6. Answers will vary. 7. She doesn't think that it will ever end. 8. They have probably increased their efforts due to the war. 9. Muslims, Croats, and Serbs 10. They have a mouse. 11. leave Sarajevo temporarily 12. No; Answers will vary.
Pages 142-168: 1. Her diary is going to be published. 2. They do not have anything to feed it. 3. run away 4. It makes her feel close to them. 5. Answers will vary. 6. She refers to her childhood as peaceful and lovely shores, and she refers to herself as a swimmer who has been forced to swim away from those shores. 7. Answers will vary. 8. Anne Frank died. 9. Cici died; Cici could cheer them all up. 10. They are trying to lift Zlata's spirits. 11. It makes the misery easier to bear.
Pages 169-197: 1. Answers will vary. 2. It is her only connection to the outside world. 3. A truce for peace is supposed to be signed. 4. So many have died and there are no more places to bury the dead. 5. 15,000 dead and 50,000 wounded 6. It doesn't happen; there is still shooting. 7. The family was to leave for Paris. 8. The personnel carrier never shows up. 9. Zlata and her family leave for Paris. 10. She is excited to see evidence of electricity and life. 11. There are still too many people without light in Sarajevo. "Whenever just some of this light illuminates the darkness in Sarajevo, then it will be my light as well."

Activities #3 & #4: Answers will vary.
Activity #5: 1. intervention 2. pedigree 3. humiliating 4. sovereign 5. liberated 6. servile 7. hernia 8. barrage
Activities #6–#16: Answers will vary.

Comprehension Quiz #1: 1. F, War is unexpected. 2. T 3. F, Zlata knows of many who are killed during the war. 4. F, Some people send their children away so that they will be safe. 5. T 6. F, In war, many who are innocent bystanders are killed. 7. T 8. F, The neighbors help and support each other. 9. F, Zlata is not allowed to play outside at all. 10. F, Mimmy was published and read all over the world.

Comprehension Quiz #2: 1. F, Zlata is somewhat able to get used to the war going on around her. 2. F, Cicko dies. 3. T 4. F, Zlata does not believe that the "kids" will come to an agreement. 5. F, Daddy doesn't think that Nedo will return from his vacation. 6. T 7. F, Zlata does not think the war will ever end. 8. F, Zlata is concerned about being compared to Anne Frank. 9. T 10. T

Final Test–
A. Short Answer: 1. She is scared to leave her loved ones, but she would love to escape the war. 2. She goes without electricity and water; she plays the piano, reads, and visits with her friends whenever possible. 3. Many of her friends have left. 4. Answers will vary. 5. no water, electricity, no baths, cold 6. They do not consider anyone other than themselves. 7. She is excited; it is a distraction from the war. 8. They lift the spirits because they allow them to forget the war for a little while; however, they celebrate with unusual gifts and must listen to the shooting surrounding them. 9. It seems as if people are accepting the situation. 10. She feels loyal to those still in Sarajevo.
B. Identification: Accept reasonable answers.
C. Essays: Use the rubric on the following page to assess student compositions.

Essay Evaluation Form

This evaluation is designed to help the teacher assess a student's essay on a 100 point scale. Circle one number (excellent/good/needs improvement) per category to get the total grade.

	Excellent	Good	Needs Improvement
1. **Focus:** The student writes a clear thesis and includes it in the opening paragraph.	10	8	4
2. **Organization:** The final draft reflects the assigned outline; transitions are used to link ideas.	20	16	12
3. **Support:** Adequate details are provided; extraneous details are omitted.	12	10	7
4. **Detail:** Each quote or reference is explained (as if the teacher had not read the book); ideas are not redundant.	12	10	7
5. **Mechanics:** Spelling, capitalization, and usage are correct.	16	12	8
6. **Sentence Structure:** The student avoids run-ons and sentence fragments.	10	8	4
7. **Verbs:** All verbs are in the correct tense; sections in which plot is summarized are in the present tense.	10	8	4
8. **Total effect of the essay**	10	8	4

Comments:

Total: __________

(This rubric may be altered to fit the needs of a particular class. You may wish to show it to students before they write their essays. They can use it as a self-evaluation tool, and they will be aware of exactly how their essays will be graded.)

Notes

